Index

Index	Page

Index

Index	Page

Index

Index	Page

Index

Index	Page

Client

Name	
Address	
Phone	
Email	
Add. info.	

Date	Time	Service	Price	Notes

Client

Name	
Address	
Phone	
Email	
Add. info.	

Date	Time	Service	Price	Notes

Client

Name	
Address	
Phone	
Email	
Add. info.	

Date	Time	Service	Price	Notes

Client

Name	
Address	
Phone	
Email	
Add. info.	

Date	Time	Service	Price	Notes

Client

Name	
Address	
Phone	
Email	
Add. info.	

Date	Time	Service	Price	Notes

Client

Name	
Address	
Phone	
Email	
Add. info.	

Date	Time	Service	Price	Notes

Client

Name	
Address	
Phone	
Email	
Add. info.	

Date	Time	Service	Price	Notes

Client

Name	
Address	
Phone	
Email	
Add. info.	

Date	Time	Service	Price	Notes

Client

Name	
Address	
Phone	
Email	
Add. info.	

Date	Time	Service	Price	Notes

Client

Name	
Address	
Phone	
Email	
Add. info.	

Date	Time	Service	Price	Notes

Client

Name	
Address	
Phone	
Email	
Add. info.	

Date	Time	Service	Price	Notes

Client

Name	
Address	
Phone	
Email	
Add. info.	

Date	Time	Service	Price	Notes

Client

Name	
Address	
Phone	
Email	
Add. info.	

Date	Time	Service	Price	Notes

Client

Name	
Address	
Phone	
Email	
Add. info.	

Date	Time	Service	Price	Notes

Client

Name	
Address	
Phone	
Email	
Add. info.	

Date	Time	Service	Price	Notes

Client

Name	
Address	
Phone	
Email	
Add. info.	

Date	Time	Service	Price	Notes

Client

Name	
Address	
Phone	
Email	
Add. info.	

Date	Time	Service	Price	Notes

Client

Name	
Address	
Phone	
Email	
Add. info.	

Date	Time	Service	Price	Notes

Client

Name	
Address	
Phone	
Email	
Add. info.	

Date	Time	Service	Price	Notes

Client

Name	
Address	
Phone	
Email	
Add. info.	

Date	Time	Service	Price	Notes

Client

Name	
Address	
Phone	
Email	
Add. info.	

Date	Time	Service	Price	Notes

Client

Name	
Address	
Phone	
Email	
Add. info.	

Date	Time	Service	Price	Notes

Client

Name	
Address	
Phone	
Email	
Add. info.	

Date	Time	Service	Price	Notes

Client

Name	
Address	
Phone	
Email	
Add. info.	

Date	Time	Service	Price	Notes

Client

Name	
Address	
Phone	
Email	
Add. info.	

Date	Time	Service	Price	Notes

Client

Name	
Address	
Phone	
Email	
Add. info.	

Date	Time	Service	Price	Notes

Client

Name	
Address	
Phone	
Email	
Add. info.	

Date	Time	Service	Price	Notes

Client

Name	
Address	
Phone	
Email	
Add. info.	

Date	Time	Service	Price	Notes

Client

Name	
Address	
Phone	
Email	
Add. info.	

Date	Time	Service	Price	Notes

Client

Name	
Address	
Phone	
Email	
Add. info.	

Date	Time	Service	Price	Notes

Client

Name	
Address	
Phone	
Email	
Add. info.	

Date	Time	Service	Price	Notes

Client

Name	
Address	
Phone	
Email	
Add. info.	

Date	Time	Service	Price	Notes

Client

Name	
Address	
Phone	
Email	
Add. info.	

Date	Time	Service	Price	Notes

Client

Name	
Address	
Phone	
Email	
Add. info.	

Date	Time	Service	Price	Notes

Client

Name	
Address	
Phone	
Email	
Add. info.	

Date	Time	Service	Price	Notes

Client

Name	
Address	
Phone	
Email	
Add. info.	

Date	Time	Service	Price	Notes

Client

Name	
Address	
Phone	
Email	
Add. info.	

Date	Time	Service	Price	Notes

Client

Name	
Address	
Phone	
Email	
Add. info.	

Date	Time	Service	Price	Notes

Client

Name	
Address	
Phone	
Email	
Add. info.	

Date	Time	Service	Price	Notes

Client

Name	
Address	
Phone	
Email	
Add. info.	

Date	Time	Service	Price	Notes

Client

Name	
Address	
Phone	
Email	
Add. info.	

Date	Time	Service	Price	Notes

Client

Name	
Address	
Phone	
Email	
Add. info.	

Date	Time	Service	Price	Notes

Client

Name	
Address	
Phone	
Email	
Add. info.	

Date	Time	Service	Price	Notes

Client

Name	
Address	
Phone	
Email	
Add. info.	

Date	Time	Service	Price	Notes

Client

Name	
Address	
Phone	
Email	
Add. info.	

Date	Time	Service	Price	Notes

Client

Name	
Address	
Phone	
Email	
Add. info.	

Date	Time	Service	Price	Notes

Client

Name	
Address	
Phone	
Email	
Add. info.	

Date	Time	Service	Price	Notes

Client

Name	
Address	
Phone	
Email	
Add. info.	

Date	Time	Service	Price	Notes

Client

Name	
Address	
Phone	
Email	
Add. info.	

Date	Time	Service	Price	Notes

Client

Name	
Address	
Phone	
Email	
Add. info.	

Date	Time	Service	Price	Notes

Client

Name	
Address	
Phone	
Email	
Add. info.	

Date	Time	Service	Price	Notes

Client

Name	
Address	
Phone	
Email	
Add. info.	

Date	Time	Service	Price	Notes

Client

Name	
Address	
Phone	
Email	
Add. info.	

Date	Time	Service	Price	Notes

Client

Name	
Address	
Phone	
Email	
Add. info.	

Date	Time	Service	Price	Notes

Client

Name	
Address	
Phone	
Email	
Add. info.	

Date	Time	Service	Price	Notes

Client

Name	
Address	
Phone	
Email	
Add. info.	

Date	Time	Service	Price	Notes

Client

Name	
Address	
Phone	
Email	
Add. info.	

Date	Time	Service	Price	Notes

Client

Name	
Address	
Phone	
Email	
Add. info.	

Date	Time	Service	Price	Notes

Client

Name	
Address	
Phone	
Email	
Add. info.	

Date	Time	Service	Price	Notes

Client

Name	
Address	
Phone	
Email	
Add. info.	

Date	Time	Service	Price	Notes

Client

Name	
Address	
Phone	
Email	
Add. info.	

Date	Time	Service	Price	Notes

Client

Name	
Address	
Phone	
Email	
Add. info.	

Date	Time	Service	Price	Notes

Client

Name	
Address	
Phone	
Email	
Add. info.	

Date	Time	Service	Price	Notes

Client

Name	
Address	
Phone	
Email	
Add. info.	

Date	Time	Service	Price	Notes

Client

Name	
Address	
Phone	
Email	
Add. info.	

Date	Time	Service	Price	Notes

Client

Name	
Address	
Phone	
Email	
Add. info.	

Date	Time	Service	Price	Notes

Client

Name	
Address	
Phone	
Email	
Add. info.	

Date	Time	Service	Price	Notes

Client

Name	
Address	
Phone	
Email	
Add. info.	

Date	Time	Service	Price	Notes

Client

Name	
Address	
Phone	
Email	
Add. info.	

Date	Time	Service	Price	Notes

Client

Name	
Address	
Phone	
Email	
Add. info.	

Date	Time	Service	Price	Notes

Client

Name	
Address	
Phone	
Email	
Add. info.	

Date	Time	Service	Price	Notes

Client

Name	
Address	
Phone	
Email	
Add. info.	

Date	Time	Service	Price	Notes

Client

Name	
Address	
Phone	
Email	
Add. info.	

Date	Time	Service	Price	Notes

Client

Name	
Address	
Phone	
Email	
Add. info.	

Date	Time	Service	Price	Notes

Client

Name	
Address	
Phone	
Email	
Add. info.	

Date	Time	Service	Price	Notes

Client

Name	
Address	
Phone	
Email	
Add. info.	

Date	Time	Service	Price	Notes

Client

Name	
Address	
Phone	
Email	
Add. info.	

Date	Time	Service	Price	Notes

Client

Name	
Address	
Phone	
Email	
Add. info.	

Date	Time	Service	Price	Notes

Client

Name	
Address	
Phone	
Email	
Add. info.	

Date	Time	Service	Price	Notes

Client

Name	
Address	
Phone	
Email	
Add. info.	

Date	Time	Service	Price	Notes

Client

Name	
Address	
Phone	
Email	
Add. info.	

Date	Time	Service	Price	Notes

Client

Name	
Address	
Phone	
Email	
Add. info.	

Date	Time	Service	Price	Notes

Client

Name	
Address	
Phone	
Email	
Add. info.	

Date	Time	Service	Price	Notes

Client

Name	
Address	
Phone	
Email	
Add. info.	

Date	Time	Service	Price	Notes

Client

Name	
Address	
Phone	
Email	
Add. info.	

Date	Time	Service	Price	Notes

Client

Name	
Address	
Phone	
Email	
Add. info.	

Date	Time	Service	Price	Notes

Client

Name	
Address	
Phone	
Email	
Add. info.	

Date	Time	Service	Price	Notes

Client

Name	
Address	
Phone	
Email	
Add. info.	

Date	Time	Service	Price	Notes

Client

Name	
Address	
Phone	
Email	
Add. info.	

Date	Time	Service	Price	Notes

Client

Name	
Address	
Phone	
Email	
Add. info.	

Date	Time	Service	Price	Notes

Client

Name	
Address	
Phone	
Email	
Add. info.	

Date	Time	Service	Price	Notes

Client

Name	
Address	
Phone	
Email	
Add. info.	

Date	Time	Service	Price	Notes

Client

Name	
Address	
Phone	
Email	
Add. info.	

Date	Time	Service	Price	Notes

Client

Name	
Address	
Phone	
Email	
Add. info.	

Date	Time	Service	Price	Notes

Client

Name	
Address	
Phone	
Email	
Add. info.	

Date	Time	Service	Price	Notes

Client

Name	
Address	
Phone	
Email	
Add. info.	

Date	Time	Service	Price	Notes

Client

Name	
Address	
Phone	
Email	
Add. info.	

Date	Time	Service	Price	Notes

Client

Name	
Address	
Phone	
Email	
Add. info.	

Date	Time	Service	Price	Notes

Client

Name	
Address	
Phone	
Email	
Add. info.	

Date	Time	Service	Price	Notes

Client

Name	
Address	
Phone	
Email	
Add. info.	

Date	Time	Service	Price	Notes

Client

Name	
Address	
Phone	
Email	
Add. info.	

Date	Time	Service	Price	Notes

Client

Name	
Address	
Phone	
Email	
Add. info.	

Date	Time	Service	Price	Notes

Client

Name	
Address	
Phone	
Email	
Add. info.	

Date	Time	Service	Price	Notes

Client

Name	
Address	
Phone	
Email	
Add. info.	

Date	Time	Service	Price	Notes

Client

Name	
Address	
Phone	
Email	
Add. info.	

Date	Time	Service	Price	Notes

Client

Name	
Address	
Phone	
Email	
Add. info.	

Date	Time	Service	Price	Notes

Made in United States
Troutdale, OR
09/28/2023

13258141R00062